PERFOR PICKLEBALL

DRILL BOOK

Over 60 pickleball drills to accelerate your performance on the courts

Includes 24 wall drills

BRETT NOEL

3X NATIONAL GOLD MEDAL WINNER

Pickleball Hall Of Fame Testimonial And National Champion Endorsement

"This compilation of skill drills is a must have and using the various drills will most certainly help you get to that next level. The importance of drilling with a purpose to achieve consistency in your game is key to success. This book makes this easier than ever by putting a multitude of drills at the tip of your finger! I highly recommend and refer to his drills book daily to my students."

Gigi LeMaster
Multi Nationals Champion
6 Time US Open Gold Medalist
Pickleball Hall of Fame Inductee 2021 / IFP| IPTPA Certified Coach

"Pickleball is not just a Sport."
"It's a way of Life."

This comprehensive guidebook will teach you a variety of pickleball drills that is both educational and fun. Helping you improve your skills with fun competitive play.

Choose from a variety of drilling sessions that can be adaptable to the number of players you have with you on the court.
The drilling and training session can be as little as ten minutes to several hours. You choose the drill, exercise and games that work for you.
In addition, I have included a variety of wall drills you can practice by yourself.

Let's Drill

A Personal Note from the Author

My name is Brett Noel, and I wrote this book for you. I am a three-time national gold medal winner and tour the world teaching pickleball to enthusiasts like you.

I have conducted hundreds of clinics and have taught thousands of players.

Prior to pickleball I had no sports background. One day a friend asked me to play pickleball and I fell in love with the sport.

I played for three hours and couldn't walk for three days. My entire body ached. Nevertheless, I knew I wanted to play more.

A few months later I received a flyer that my local community park was teaching pickleball and I signed up immediately. Though the instructor meant well, much of what was taught was incorrect. **I had to unlearn a lot of bad habits**.

I became a competitive player and in a few short years I won my first gold medal at nationals. I defended that title again and again, walking away as a three time national gold medal winner.

I share this not to impress you but to impress upon you that if I can become a national champion with no sports background, you can improve your game and get to the next level by implementing what I am going to teach you.

I want to save you years of trial and error and get you on the fast track to success.

Everything I teach in this book I have done myself. I will share with you the mindset of a champion and show how you can become a better player.

I am not an author. In fact, I think English was my worst subject. I write the way I talk, and you might find some grammatical errors in this book, and it may not be perfect. It was created from me to you from the heart.

I am often asked, "How are you"? My response is always the same. I woke up in the body. If you wake up in the body, it is a good day. **If you woke up in the body and get to play pickleball, "It's a great day".**

The #1 Problem in Pickleball is

The Ball

Be the last player to hit the ball over the over the net

Most players hit the ball with the hope of just getting it over the net.

I call this "Hit and Pray." You need to move from "Hit and Pray" to hitting with purpose.

We start with dinking exercises designed to give you more control at the kitchen line, setting yourself up for more winning shots and forcing your opponents to make unforced errors.

The game of pickleball has changed over the years from dinking back and forth, waiting for your opponent to make a mistake, to dinking with purpose and direction forcing your opponent to make a mistake.

The purpose of dinking is to irritate your opponents. How do you irritate your opponents? You make them move stretch and reach. You make them bend.

The more you make your opponent's move, stretch, and reach for the ball, the more likely they will make an unforced error.

The more they reach and bend the less likely they can attack you.

For dinks to be effective, they need to be more linear. That means that the path of the ball needs to be straighter and have less of an arc.

As I teach drills and strategies throughout this book, I will refer to three types of arcs in pickleball.

The three arcs I refer to in pickleball is the "McDonalds Arc", the "St Louis Missouri Arc" and a "Pickleball Arc".

When dinking, I want you to focus on the "Pickleball Arc"

3 arcs in pickleball

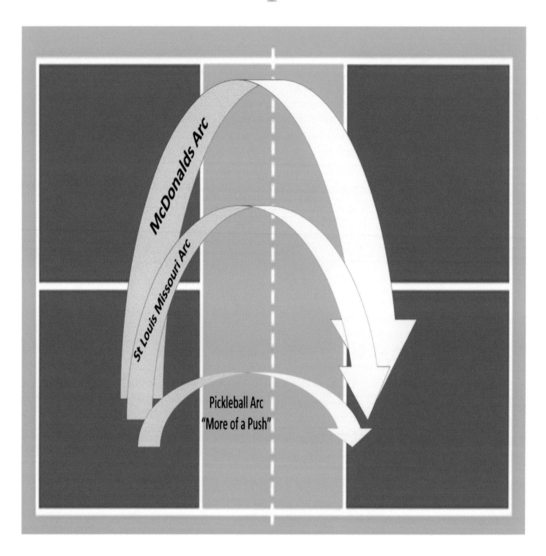

McDonalds Arc

St Louis Missouri Arc

Pickleball Arc
"More of a Push"

The best target areas to attack when dinking

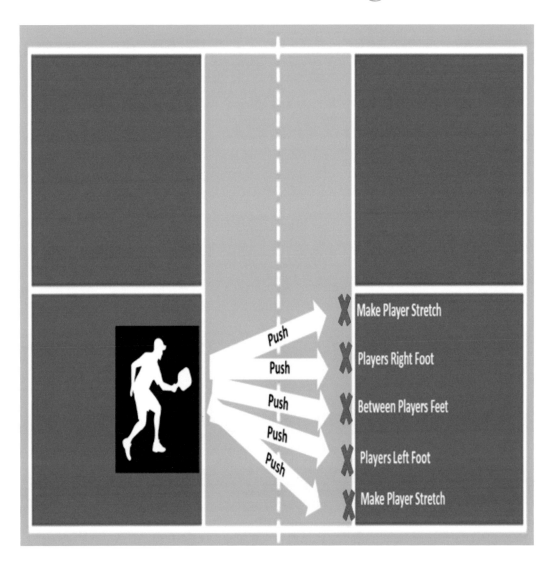

DRILL #1 Moving them around

Both players stand at the kitchen line dinking to each other. Make sure you are balanced when you hit the ball? You should be using your shoulder keeping your elbow and wrist firm and locked in.

After hitting the ball make sure you raise your paddle back to ready position. Expect every ball to come back hard and fast.

The goal is to hit the ball over the net consistently trying to move your opponent around. Make them move reach and stretch.

Think of these key areas.

1. After hitting the ball, remember to get your paddle up. Do not let it hang at your waist or hip.
2. Remember not to back swing or accelerate as you hit the ball. Simply drop your paddle and push the ball over the net.
3. Hit the ball in a direction that forces your opponent to move and stretch.

As you dink back and forth, focus on the direction of the ball as well as the height of the ball. If the ball is too high, lower your arc.

Hint: The ball will go in the direction of your palm.

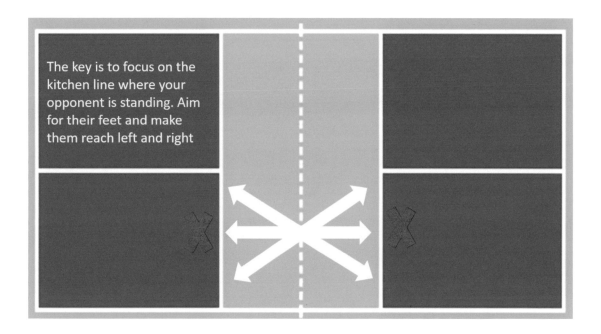

The key is to focus on the kitchen line where your opponent is standing. Aim for their feet and make them reach left and right

DRILL #2 Hitting with Purpose

Focusing on the Sideline

As you dink back and forth, focus on the direction of the ball as well as the height of the ball.

Hint: The ball will go in the direction of your palm. Your palm becomes the navigator. If your palm pushes towards your opponent's left foot, the ball will go in the direction of their left foot.

Targeting the sideline is a great way to force your opponent to pop up the ball. Especially if you can get the ball behind them. The goal when targeting the sideline is to get the ball behind them. Pushing the ball down the line.

During drill number one we were practicing pushing our dinks with direction and purpose. We were mixing up our shots. This drill is about adding weapons to your arsenal by attacking down the line.

Your goal is to make them stretch and reach for the ball as it is about to pass them. By focusing on hitting the ball down the line, you are isolating your opponent.

When you dink down the sidelines, their partner must move over to cover their partners exposed area and that opens more of the court for you and your partner to attack.

If their partner does not move over to cover the exposed area, the middle of the court opens and can be attacked. Both players are at the kitchen line. Each player hitting in the same direction towards the side-line of the court.

If both players are right- handed, then one player will be returning with their forehand and the other player will be returning with their backhand. Warm up for five minutes then play competitive rally score to five points. Win by one point. Ernes are allowed during competitive play.

It is important to drill on both sides of the court. One side will be your forehand and the other will be your backhand. **We are creating muscle memory.** Make sure you shift and drill from both sides.

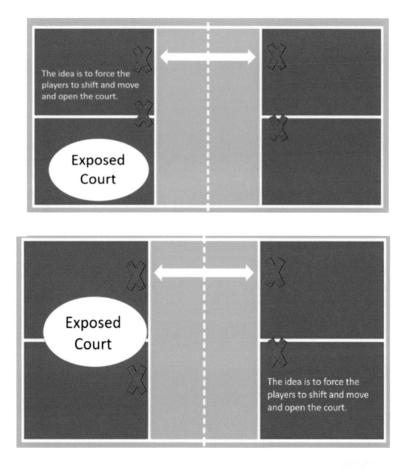

DRILL #3 Hitting with Purpose

Aim for the Middle

A concept that I want to introduce to you, and I want you to be aware of on the court are angles. If we can cut off the angles, the highest probability shot will be straight. Allowing you to expect their next shot.

In this drill we are keeping the ball towards the center of the court reducing effective angle shots. When the ball is in the center of the court, any angle shot your opponent hits needs to be soft or it will go out of the court.

Both players are at the kitchen line. Each player hitting in the same direction. Towards the center of the court.

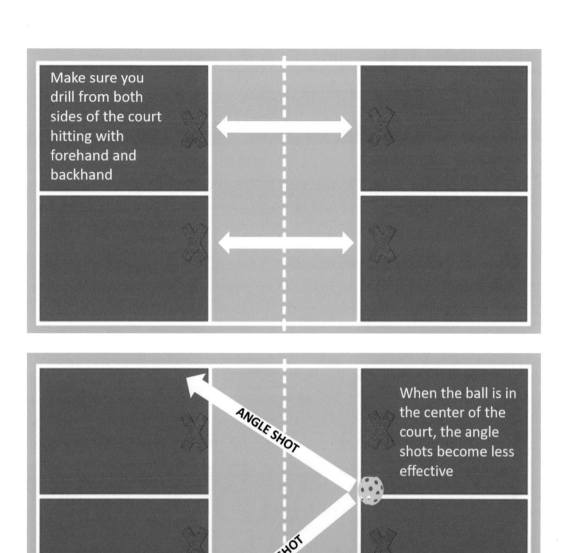

Make sure you drill from both sides of the court hitting with forehand and backhand

ANGLE SHOT

ANGLE SHOT

When the ball is in the center of the court, the angle shots become less effective

DRILL #4 Cross Court Dinking

Backhand to Backhand

There are three major benefits to dinking cross court.

1. You have ten more feet of error room
2. You are hitting over the lowest part of the net
3. You put the ball in front of your partner, and it becomes two against one.

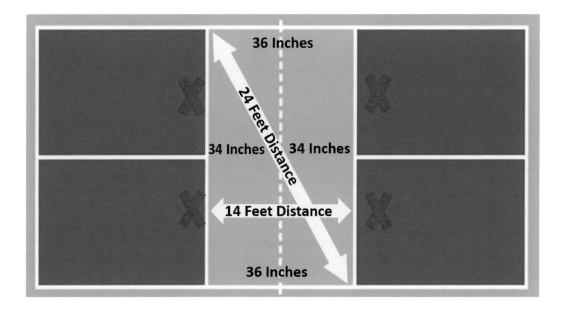

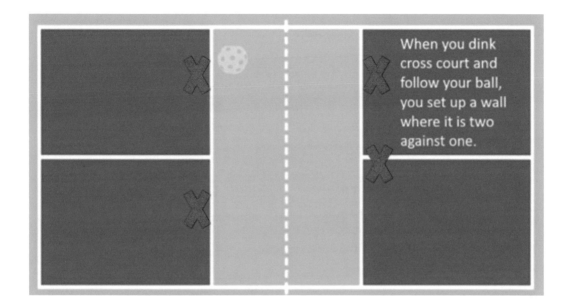

When you dink cross court and follow your ball, you set up a wall where it is two against one.

Both players are at the kitchen line. Each player hitting in the same direction which is across from their opponent. If both players are right- handed, then both players will be returning with their backhands.

Most dinking should be with your backhand. Focus on returning dinks with your backhand unless the ball is to the right side of your foot.

Backhand to Backhand

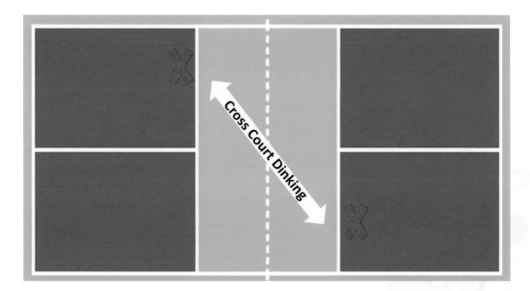

Cross Court Dinking

DRILL #5 Cross Court Dinking

Forehand to Forehand

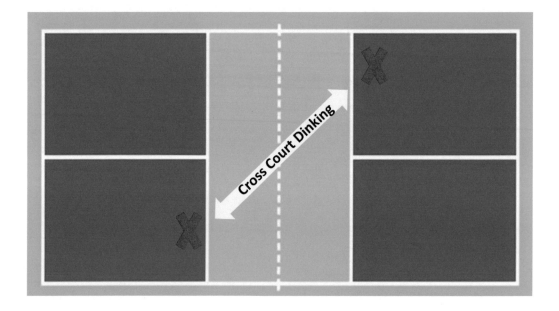

One of the common mistakes players make when practicing cross court dinks is to stand and stay at the sidelines.

If you dink cross court, then you must follow your ball. After hitting the ball step towards the center of the court. This cuts off your opponent's ability to attack down the middle.

DRILL #6 Hitting with Purpose

Right Leg Left leg.

Start off facing each other dinking back and forth. Instead of just hitting the ball and praying that it goes over the net. **Start to hit with purpose.**

Begin by hitting the ball to your partner's right leg. They in turn will hit the ball to your right leg. Your next shot is to their left leg. They will return the ball to your left leg as well. Continue hitting back and forth to your partner in this manner.

You are learning to target certain areas within the kitchen area. You are hitting with purpose and direction. **Make sure you use your shoulder when striking the ball.**

Hint: The ball will go where your palm goes. If your palm goes to their left leg, the ball will go to their left leg. When hitting a backhand, it will be your knuckles that lead the ball.

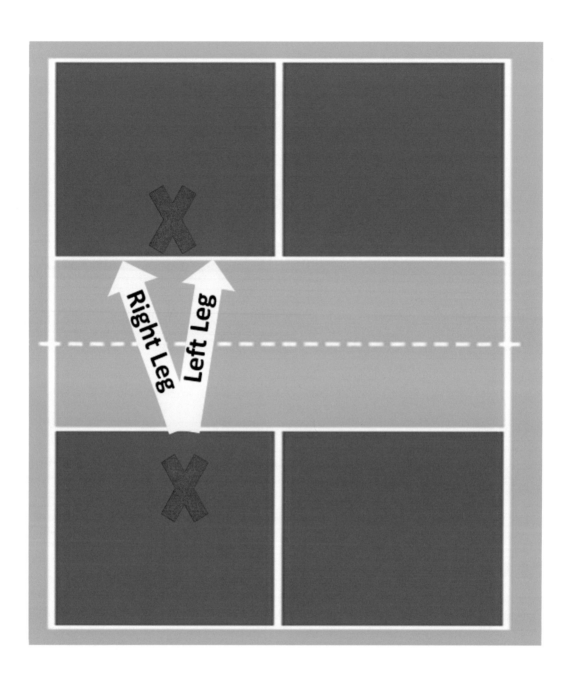

DRILL #7 Hitting with Purpose

Target Dinking

In this drill three different colored markers are placed on one side of the net. One player will start by calling a color and your opponent needs to return the ball to the area of that specific color.

Make sure you shout out the color of the marker before you hit the ball over the net. After a while, change sides and your partner now calls which color marker, he or she wants you to hit to.

Try and move your partner around within the ten feet of the court making them reach, stretch, and move.

Remember to use your shoulder when dinking and focus to push the ball in the direction of the color that was called.

Be more linear with your dinks as you hit the ball in the chosen direction.

As mentioned before, the ball will go in the direction of your palm on forehands and knuckles on your backhand.

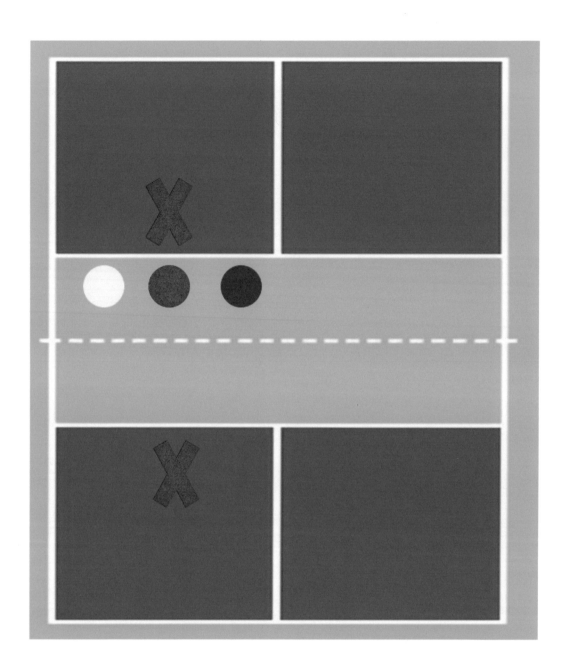

DRILL #8 Hitting with Purpose

Zone Dinking

In this specific exercise you are taking dinking to the next level. Each player takes their position at the non-volley zone. Break down the kitchen area into four quadrants. They are marked quadrant number 1, 2, 3, and 4.

You can mark these quadrants with court tape, or you can place color cones in each section. One player will call out the quadrant that they want their opponent to hit the ball to.

Another option is to try and hit each quadrant in order. Start hitting to quadrant one than two than three than four. You can also start on quadrant four than three than two and finally one. Just have fun with it.

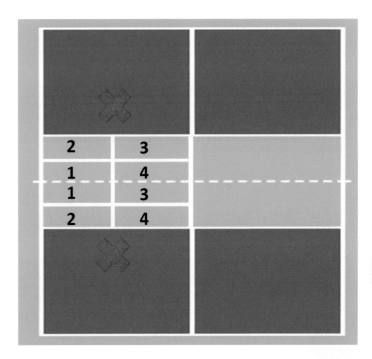

DRILL #9 Hitting with Purpose

Slinky Drill

One person will stay at the kitchen line and the other player will hit a few dinks into the kitchen then take a small step backwards.

Always return the ball into the kitchen. The person staying at the kitchen line is always hitting the ball back to the other players feet no matter where they are on the court.

By placing the ball at your opponent's feet, you are practicing your fourth shot in pickleball, keeping them back.

Your partner will slowly work their way to the baseline and then back to the kitchen. Then it is your turn to slowly work your way to the base line and back up to the kitchen line.

You are practicing drop shots from anywhere on the court as well as your fourth shot in pickleball. You can practice this drill with two or four players.

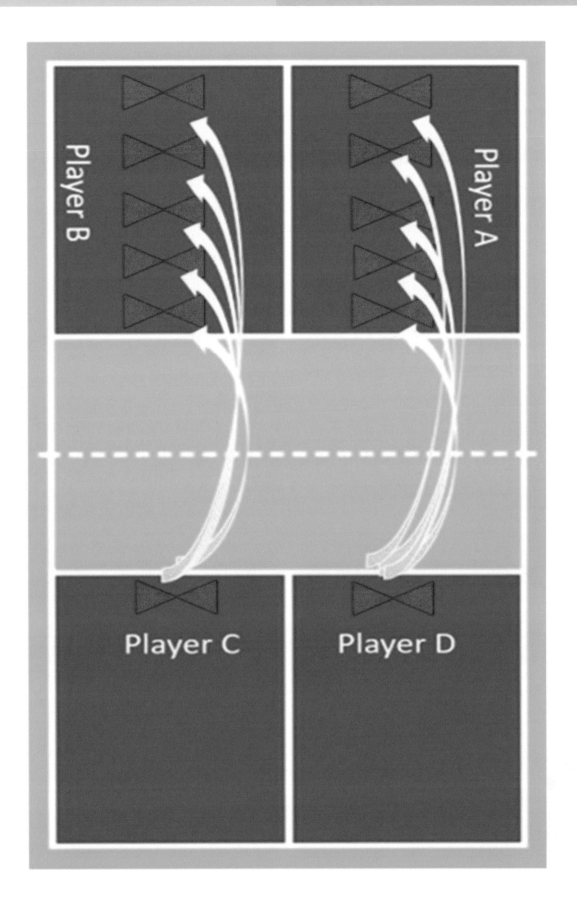

DRILL #10 Hitting with Purpose

Around The World
Hitting with purpose around the world

One player will stay at the kitchen line hitting the ball to his partner as they move around the court. The player moving around the court gets to practice hitting a soft return shot to a specific area in the kitchen.

Round one is the right side of the court into the kitchen. Round two is to the center of the court and round three is the opposite side of the court. This drill benefits both the person at the kitchen line as well as the player hitting from nine different spots on the court.

Complete your pattern and work your way back up to where you started. The player at the kitchen line is practicing their 4th shot and keeping their opponent back.

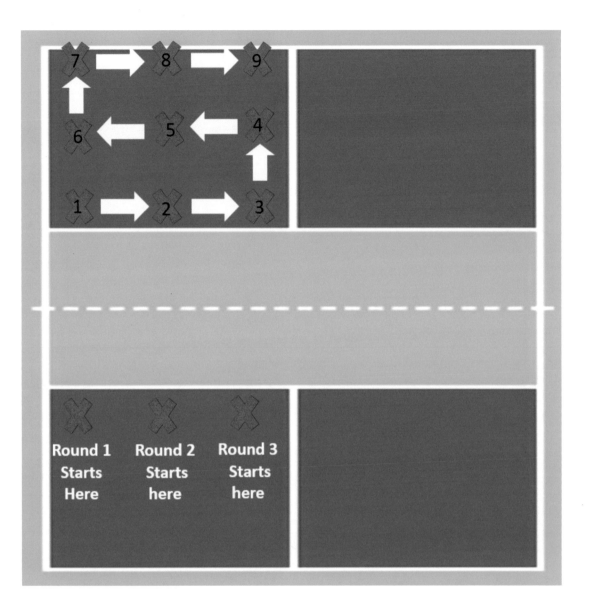

DRILL #11 Hitting with Purpose

Attacking from the Kitchen

Dinking is no longer about waiting for the opponent to make a mistake. It is about forcing your opponent to make mistakes and creating an opportunity to attack.

Both players stay at the kitchen line. Each player dinks to each other waiting for an opportunity to attack. Your attack must be disguised as a dink and at the last moment the ball is flicked or pushed straight into the opponent.

In this drill, player A will be the only one attacking. Player B will defend only. Drill for five minutes, then switch roles. After working on this drill with only one side attacking, change it up. Dink to each other where either player can attack at any time.

Note: This is a fantastic opportunity to practice blocking and resetting for the player that is defending.

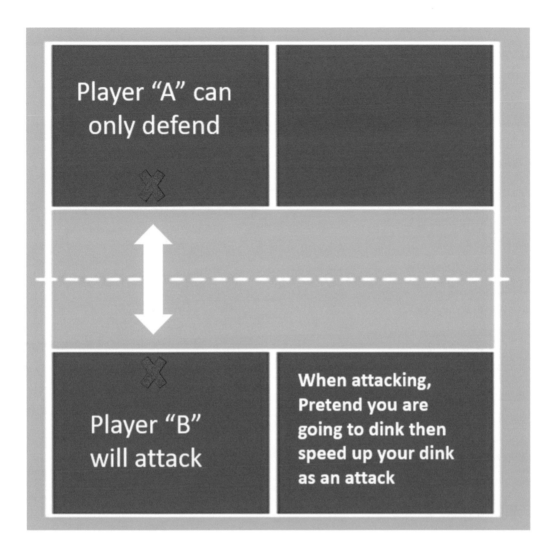

DRILL #12 Hitting with Purpose

Volley Dinking — Aim for the Cones

One of the most common issues I see with pickleball players when dinking is moving backwards for no apparent reason.

I often ask, "Why are you moving back, you are not in danger". There is a time to move back from the kitchen line, but too often players are moving backwards and allowing their opponent more time to reset and get prepared. **By moving backwards unnecessarily, you lose the opportunity to attack.**

In this drill both players place cones on the inside of the kitchen, about twelve to twenty-four inches. **The goal is for each player to dink to one another trying to hit the cones.**

No player is allowed to back up. That means you will have to take balls out of the air. This drill is all about taking dink volleys.

Remember: Most dinks are with your backhand. Including volley dinks.

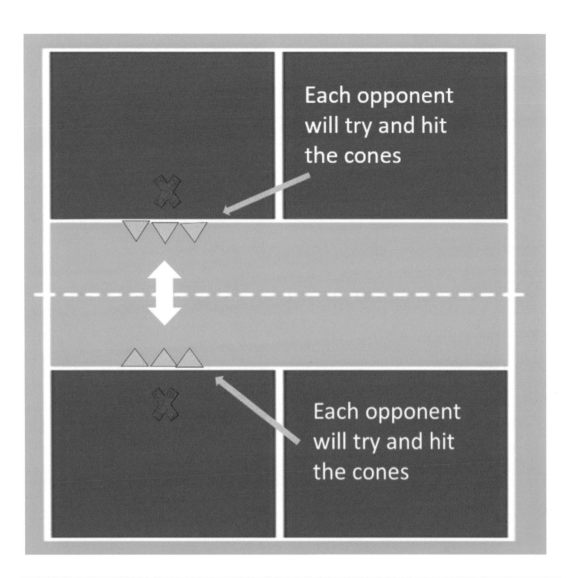

Each opponent will try and hit the cones

Each opponent will try and hit the cones

DRILL #13 Volley at the kitchen line with direction

Both players are at the kitchen line. Each player hitting a controlled volley to each other. Practice hitting with both forehand and backhand.

Each player hitting in the same direction. Towards the side-line of the court. If both players are right- handed, one player will be returning with their forehand and the other player will be returning with their backhand.

We are creating muscle memory. When you are dinking and your opponent gives a higher ball you can attack down the line with a forehand or backhand.

One of the key components in volleys is balance. Make sure you are well balanced when hitting the ball. Make sure that you are using your shoulders and not just your wrist or elbow when striking the ball.

Make sure your paddle is up and in front.

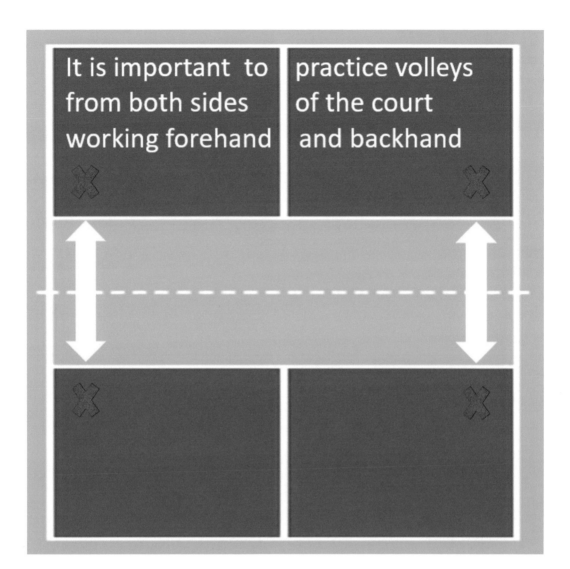

It is important to practice volleys from both sides of the court working forehand and backhand

DRILL #14 Volley at the kitchen line

Mid court with direction

Both players are at the kitchen line. Each player hitting a controlled volley to their opponent. Each player hitting in the same direction. Towards the middle of the court.

If both players are right- handed, then one player will be returning with their forehand and the other player will be returning with their backhand.

One of the key components in volleys is balance. Make sure you are well balanced when hitting the ball. Make sure that you are using your shoulders and not just your wrist or elbow when striking the ball.

Note: This is a great drill because many of your attacks will be from mid court. Your opponent gives you a little higher ball than they like. Instead of dinking it over, you attack.

Volley in a straight line. If both players are right-handed, then one will be hitting forehands and the other backhands.

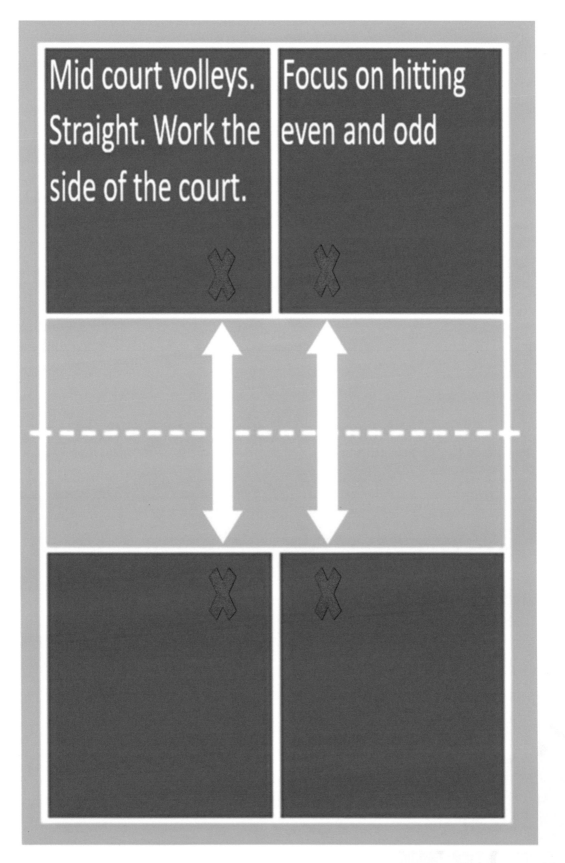

Mid court volleys. Straight. Work the side of the court.

Focus on hitting even and odd

DRILL #15 Volley at the kitchen line

Mid court mix it up

Both players are at the kitchen line. Each player hitting anywhere at their opponent. The volley can be to their forehand, backhand or to the middle.

The key is to move your opponent around. If you get pulled out of position, make sure you get back into proper position as soon as possible.

Important: When hitting a volley, the common mistake players make is following through and bringing your paddle across your body.

You have to expect that the ball will be coming back and you need to have your paddle in the ready position.

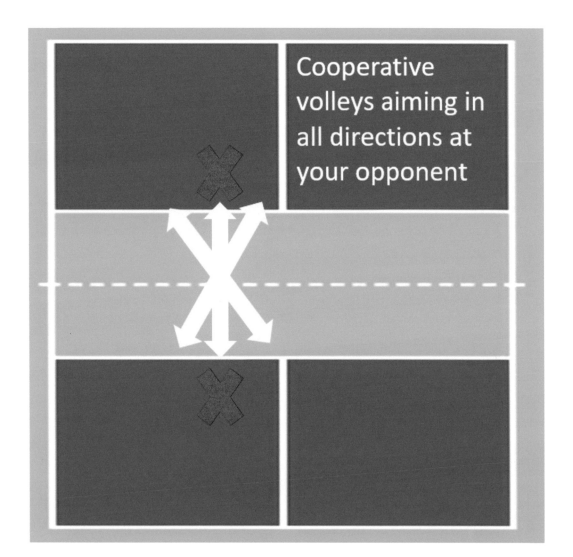

Cooperative volleys aiming in all directions at your opponent

DRILL #16 Roll Volleys

Top Spin Volley

Both players are at the kitchen line. In this exercise the goal is to dink where your partner can take the ball out of the air. Rather than dink the ball out of the air the goal is to speed up the ball with a roll volley.

A roll volley is a more aggressive hit where the ball is returned faster with more speed. The topspin allows you to hit the ball harder where the ball will stay in the court. This exercise teaches the player to relax their wrist and volley back even if the ball is below the net.

If feeding the ball is difficult, you can toss the ball with your hand. When rolling the volley, drop the tip of your paddle down towards six o'clock position and roll upwards toward eleven o'clock. **Remember to relax your wrist and strike in a forward motion as if you were swatting a fly away from you.**

The roll volley can be with your forehand or backhand.

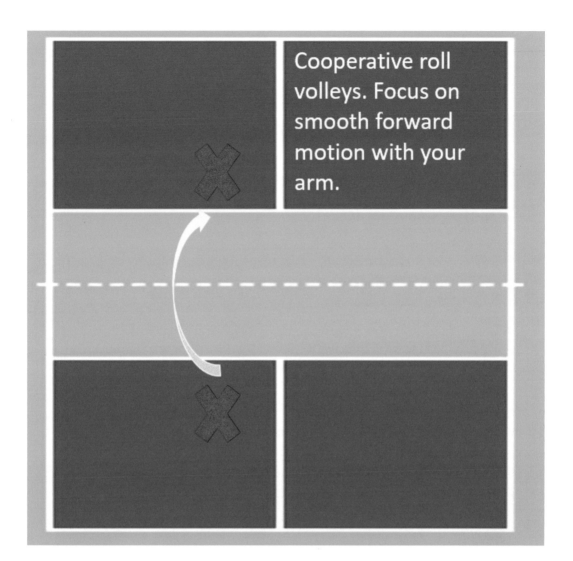

Cooperative roll volleys. Focus on smooth forward motion with your arm.

DRILL #17 Working in the Transition Area

One player will stand in mid-court (No longer called "No man's land but called "Opportunity land")

In this exercise one player is trying to get the ball back into the kitchen. The other player is to keep the ball back to mid court, ideally at their feet. Volley back when the opportunity is there. Practice your top spin volleys keeping your opponent back in mid court.

It the ball is high enough and you can attack from mid court, do it.

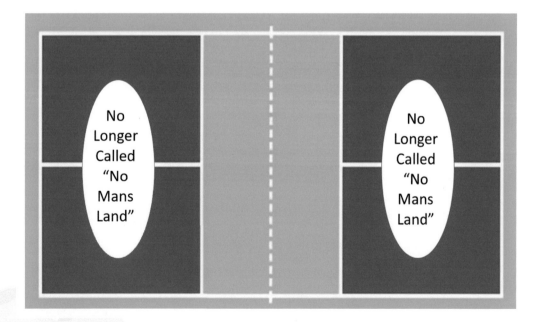

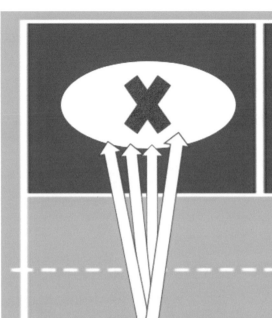

Stay in this area where you will block, reset, and <u>counter attack</u>

Make your opponent stretch for the ball

Your goal at the kitchen line is to keep the ball at your opponent's feet

DRILL #18 Defending from Baseline attacks

One player will stay at the kitchen line. The other player will stand behind the baseline and drive balls. In this exercise the player standing behind the baseline is to drive the ball at the player standing at the kitchen.

For effective and consistent drives, make sure you are driving at about 60-70%. The player at the kitchen will practice block volleys, punch volleys and letting out balls go out.

This exercise accomplishes two primary goals. The first goal is to reduce the fear players have from players that drive, (bangers) and to build their confidence in blocking and returning hard drives.

It also allows one player to practice and develop good groundstrokes.

Your paddle should be in ready position. Most of your blocks and volleys will be with your backhand.

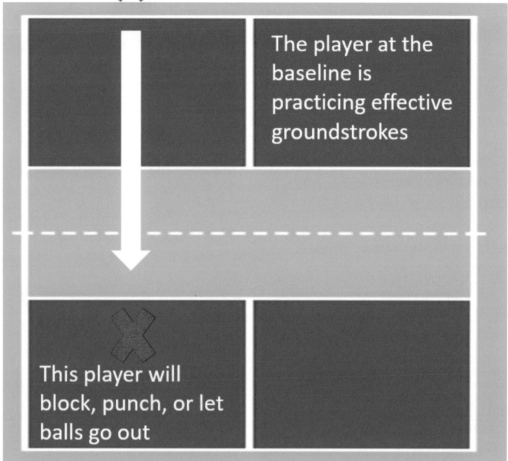

The player at the baseline is practicing effective groundstrokes

This player will block, punch, or let balls go out

DRILL #19 Drops from baseline and practicing your fourth shot

One player will stay at the kitchen line. The other player will stand behind the baseline. In this exercise the goal of the player standing behind the baseline is to drop the ball back into the kitchen in front of player. Try not to let the player at the kitchen return your ball out of the air.

The player at the kitchen is returning deep to the baseline preventing them from getting to the net.

In essence the player at the kitchen is practicing their fourth shot (rarely discussed but vitally important). The fourth shot is about keeping your opponent from getting to the kitchen line.

You can have fun with this drill. Set some goals for yourself, like getting four drops into the kitchen in a row.

If you keep your paddle up in ready position and drop your paddle to execute, you will find your thirds are more consistent and effective.

The goal is to drop into the kitchen not allowing the ball to be hit out of the air

This player will return the ball deep to the baseline

BASELINE DRILLS

DRILL #20 Hit & Move / Hit & Move

One of the most important skills sets you can develop is "Hit and Move". Too many players are hitting the ball, admiring their shot, or hitting and judging whether to move forward or not.

You will be right 80% of the time to hit and move. It's so much easier to hit and move then to hit and judge. The good news is that you will recognize how bad the other 20% shots are and not move forward.

It is important to understand that the concept is not "Drive and Dash" or Drop and Dash". How many times have we been yelled at to get to the line NOW!?

Sometimes all we can get to, is the middle of the court. This drill is about hitting from the baseline, moving to the middle of the court, and hitting, then advancing to the kitchen line to start dinking.

Take your time advancing. You should always stop and split step before our opponent is about to hit the ball.

48

Step 1. Drop from the baseline into the kitchen and move to the middle of the court into the kitchen

Step 2. Drop from midcourt into the kitchen and move to the line.

Step 3. Start a dinking rally

Your goal is to always get the ball to their feet

DRILL #21 Bounce and volley lobs

In this drill you are practicing lobs from the kitchen line. Both players are at the kitchen line dinking to each other waiting for the opportunity to lob.

Whether the ball bounces first or you lob off the volley, the technique is the same. Make sure you do not telegraph the lob. Your opponent should be thinking you are going to dink when your arm extends higher for a lob.

A good time to lob is when your opponent is off balance or out of position. Look at their footing. Are they planted on their heels and unable to move quickly.

If your opponent's paddle is down low, you might have a good opportunity to lob.

After a few minutes, each player will rotate positions, so each has an opportunity to lob from the kitchen line.

Make sure you have plenty of balls to practice with, you will be lobbying a lot!!

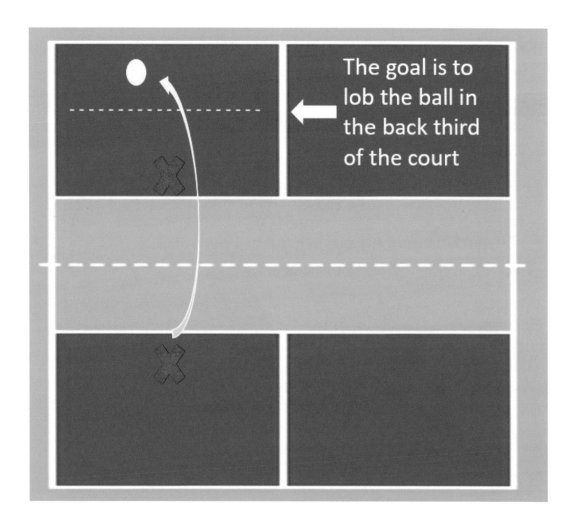

The goal is to lob the ball in the back third of the court

DRILL #22 Lobs from the kitchen with three players

This lob drill is ideal with three players and emulates a real game. Instead of the partner chasing down the lob, they will wait at the baseline.

Two players will be at the kitchen line and one at the baseline. The two players at the kitchen will dink until one player lobs.

When the one player is lobbed, he or she will move off the court. The player at the baseline will pretend they chased the lob down and will return the ball trying to work their way to the kitchen line.

The two players will play out the point as if it was a real game. The two players on the same side of the court will rotate positions and after a few minutes will rotate to be the player lobbing.

Note: Most players do not like being lobbed and this immediately puts them on the defensive. This is a good skill to have when attacking from the kitchen.

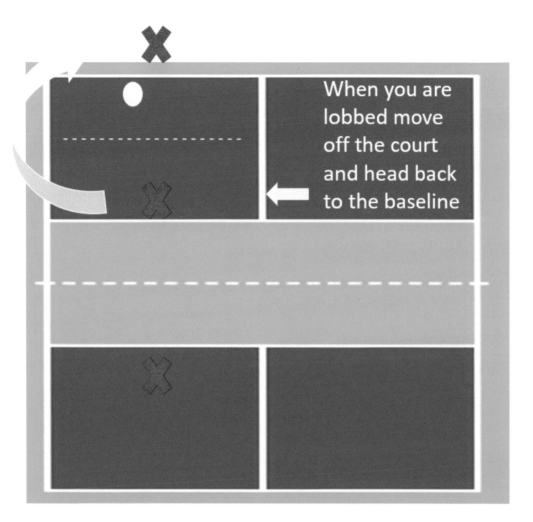

When you are lobbed move off the court and head back to the baseline

DRILL #23 Serves as a weapon

The purpose of the serve is to set up your third shot. Ideally you want your opponent to return their serve short, as in the middle of the court.

The first rule in serving is to get it in. After being able to consistently get your serve in, the next goal is to serve deep. After serving deep consistently start to serve with direction.

Learn to serve to your opponent's backhand, forehand and directly at them.

In this drill set cones to the area you are serving and start to practice with direction. Practice serving to the backhand, forehand and center.

No matter what direction you are serving to, the location should be in the back third of the court.

The ideal situation would be to force your opponent to return serve from behind the baseline.

Good serves can be worth four or five points every game, depending on your skill level. Don't forget to practice your lob serves.

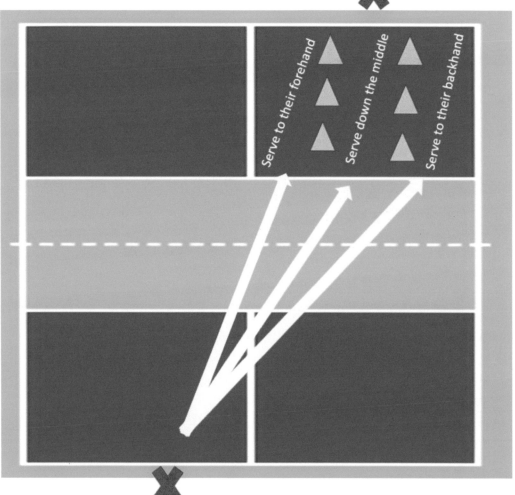

DRILL #24 Punch Volley – Play it out Two or Four Players

This is a great drill to help you defeat bangers.

One player will start at the kitchen line and other will start at the baseline. The player at the kitchen will feed an easy ball to the player at the baseline who will drive the ball at you.

The player at the kitchen line will return the ball with a punch volley and play out the point. Use only half of the court if two players.

After a while, the player at the baseline will move to the non-volley zone and those at the non-volley zone will move back to the baseline.

You can practice this drill with four players. You will find quickly that the forehand does not always get the ball in the middle.

One common mistake many players make is assuming the forehand always gets the middle. This is not true.

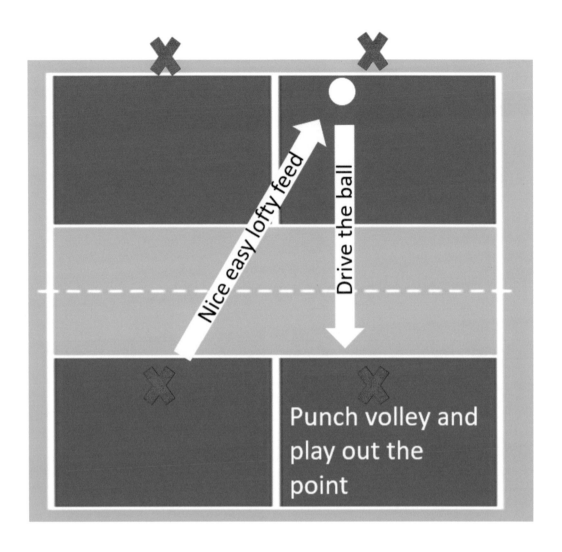

DRILL #25 Prepare for the overhead smash

Two or four players

Occasionally, a player will pop up the ball and the opponent will attack with an overhead smash.

Both players will retreat and prepare to defend a fast-approaching ball.

"Overhead Smash Defense Technique". In this drill two players will start at the kitchen line and two will start at the baseline.

The players at the kitchen line will hit an overhead smash either to a single player or between the players at the baseline.

The players at the baseline will defend the smash and return the ball and all players will play out the point.

This drill creates great defensive skills when dealing with overhead smashes. After a while, the players at the baseline will move to the kitchen line and those at the kitchen line will move back to the baseline.

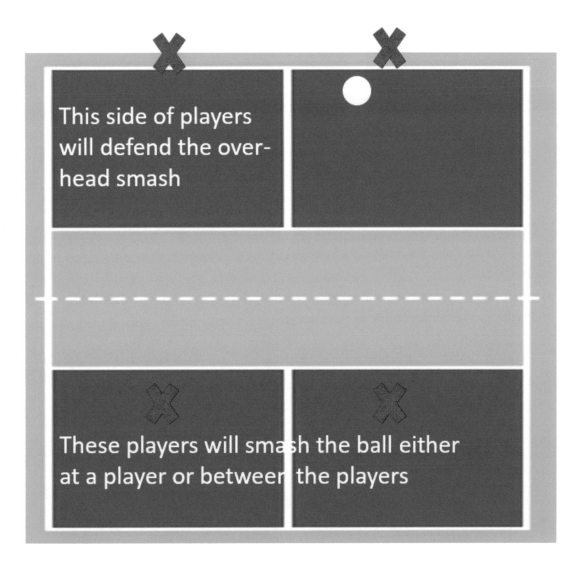

This side of players will defend the over-head smash

These players will smash the ball either at a player or between the players

VOLLEY DRILL WITH FOUR PLAYERS

DRILL #26 Aggressive volleys from the kitchen

All four players start at the kitchen line. One player starts the volley, and each player can hit the ball anywhere in the kitchen area. It must be a volley.

Once a mistake is made by hitting the ball into the net or a bad volley, each player will rotate positions.

This allows players to practice their volleys from all positions on the court.

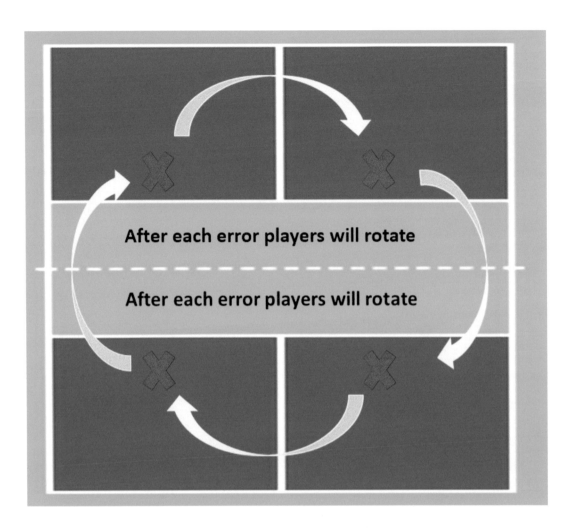

After each error players will rotate

After each error players will rotate

DRILL #27 Crazy 8 Volleys

I call this drill the crazy 8 Volley drill because the ball is traveling in a crazy eight rotation. One side (Two players) will always be hitting the ball straight ahead and the opposing side (two players) will always be hitting the ball cross court.

This creates a "Crazy 8" pattern.

After a few rotations change direction of the ball. Those players that were hitting straight ahead will now hit cross court. Those that were hitting cross court will now hit straight ahead.

Once a mistake is made by hitting the ball into the net or a bad volley, rotate positions. This develops the skill set to hit a volley to a certain location when an opportunity arises.

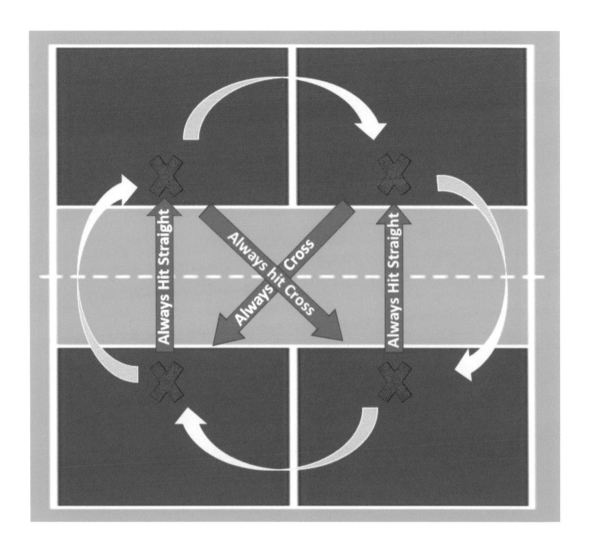

DRILL #28 Two or four players Transition Development

In this exercise one player will stand at the kitchen line and one will stand in the middle of the court.

The player at the kitchen line will feed the ball to the player in the middle of the court , who will either drop it into the kitchen or drive the ball.

The person at the kitchen line is practicing keeping the opponent back by attacking their opponents' feet with the ball.

The player in the middle of the court is practicing soft drops, blocks, hard drives, and counter attacks.

What separates the lower-level players from the rest is defense. The ability to execute shots from the transition area will make the difference in your ability to advance as a player.

One main difference between better players is the ability to perform in the transition area.

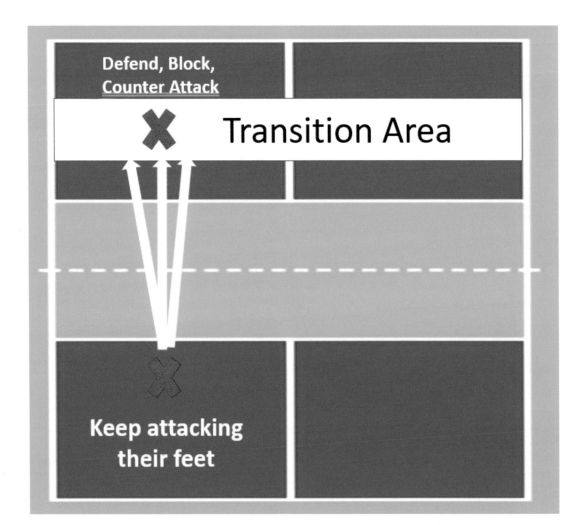

DRILL #29 Two or Four players Opportunity land/Game On

In this exercise two players will stand at the kitchen line and two will stand in the middle of the court.

The players at the kitchen line will feed the ball to those standing in the middle of the court. The feed should be soft, easy, and attackable.

The players starting in the middle of the court play the ball as in a real game. They can drop it, drive it, or lob it. It is "Game on" Play the point out. Hit and move.

You can play five points and then switch roles, or you can play the game where the winner of the point moves to the middle of the court.

Either way is fun. It develops your ability to keep opponents from moving towards the kitchen line when they are in the transition area.

Those players in the middle of the court are working on good shot that allows them to move forward to the kitchen line.

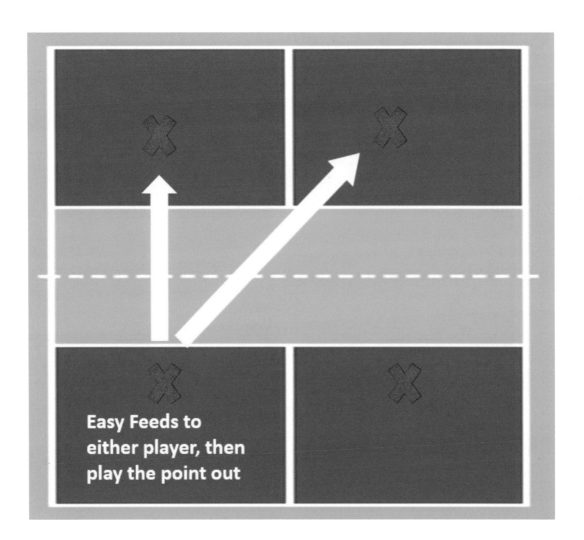

Easy Feeds to either player, then play the point out

DRILL #30 Point / Counter Point

2 or 4 Players can practice this Drill. One side will start serving and the other side will return serve. The goal is to serve, and return serve within the back one-third of the court. You can mark the courts to establish targets.

If the server gets the serve in the area, they score a point. If the return server also lands in the designated area, they counter the point, and no score is allowed.

If the server gets the ball in the designated area and the return server does not hit the mark, the server gets the point (There was no counter Point). This is a great drill to practice deep serves and deep returns. First person to eleven wins.

The purpose of the serve is to set up your third shot. You are trying to force your opponent to hit a shallow return of serve, ideally in the middle of the court.

Ideally, you want the opponent to return the serve from behind the baseline. You can achieve this by hitting deep serves.

Note: You do not have to hit harder to get the serve deep. Raise the arc of the ball for added depth.

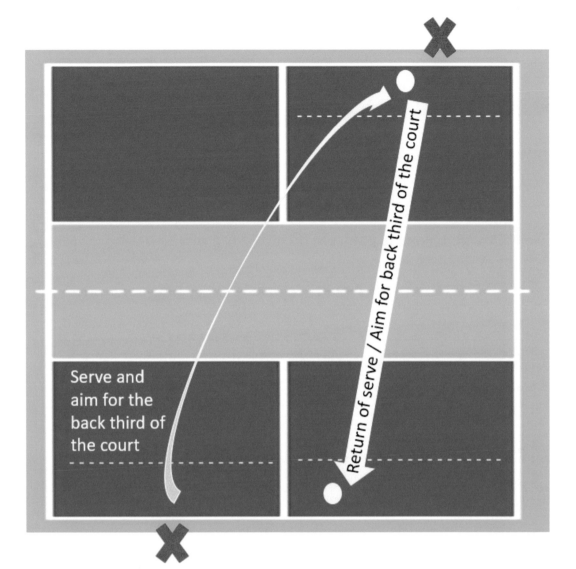

Serve and aim for the back third of the court

Return of serve / Aim for back third of the court

DRILL #31 Serve / Return Serve / Drop

In this drill the server will attempt to serve deep. The receiver will attempt to return deep. The goal is for the server to do a third shot drop in the kitchen.

Do not try and play the point out after the third shot. This drill allows the server to practice deep serves and third shot drops into the kitchen.

It allows the other player to practice deep return of serves. Notice how difficult it is to execute a good third shot drop when the return of serve is deep.

To make this drill more fun, use a trash can. A standard 32-gallon trash can will work great. The goal is to get your third shots drops to land inside the trash can.

You can move the trash can around in different areas of the kitchen to practice specific target areas.

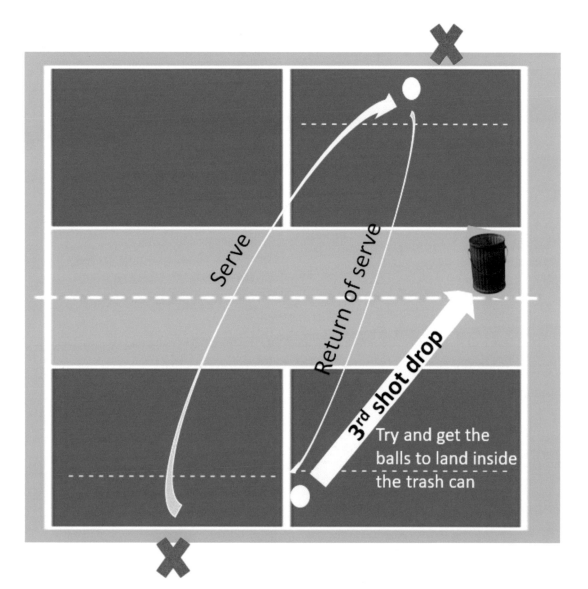

Serve

Return of serve

3rd shot drop

Try and get the
balls to land inside
the trash can

DRILL #32 Three or four players

This is a dinking drill where all players benefit. Player "A" can dink to any player on the opposite side of the court.

Players "B. C. D" must always dink back to player "A." Player "A" has the option of staying in one place or moving across the non-volley zone line.

Play out several points and then rotate positions in a clockwise order. Player "A" will take player "B's" spot and player "D" will take player "A's" spot. Keep rotating until all players hit from the single side of the court.

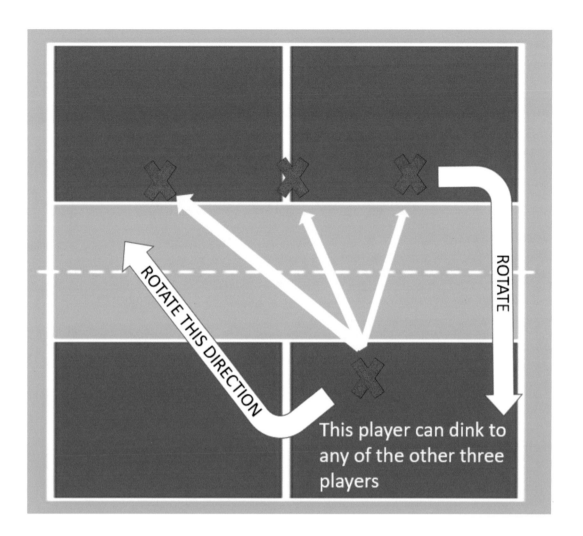

ROTATE THIS DIRECTION

ROTATE

This player can dink to any of the other three players

DRILL #33 Straight ground strokes Cross court ground strokes

Two Players

Both players will stay at the baseline practicing groundstrokes deep in their opponent's territory.

To get the ball deeper you do not need to hit it harder. You just need to increase the arc of the ball.

One of the most effective ways to execute a good ground stroke is preparation. Your body should be facing the ball (Hunt the ball) and your paddle should be up in front of you in ready position.

As soon as you see the trajectory of the ball coming towards you, get prepared. Drop your paddle and move towards the ball.

One of the biggest mistakes players make is waiting for the ball to bounce before they drop their paddle. This lack of preparation causes players to rush the ball and execute less than effective drives.

In this drill, you will practice straight groundstrokes and cross court ground strokes.

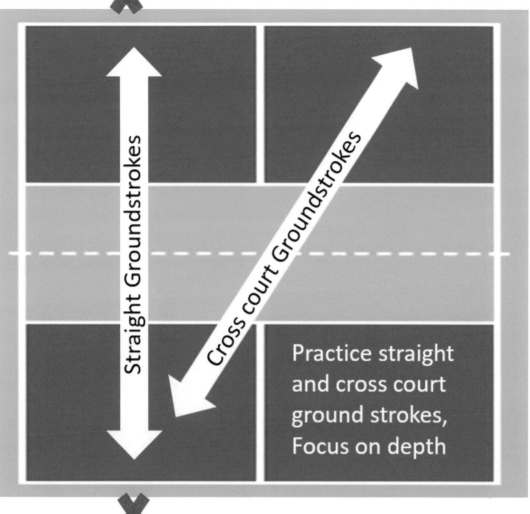

Straight Groundstrokes

Cross court Groundstrokes

Practice straight and cross court ground strokes, Focus on depth

DRILL #34 Crazy 8 Format

4 Players

In this drill two players will hit straight groundstrokes, and the other side will hit cross court groundstrokes..

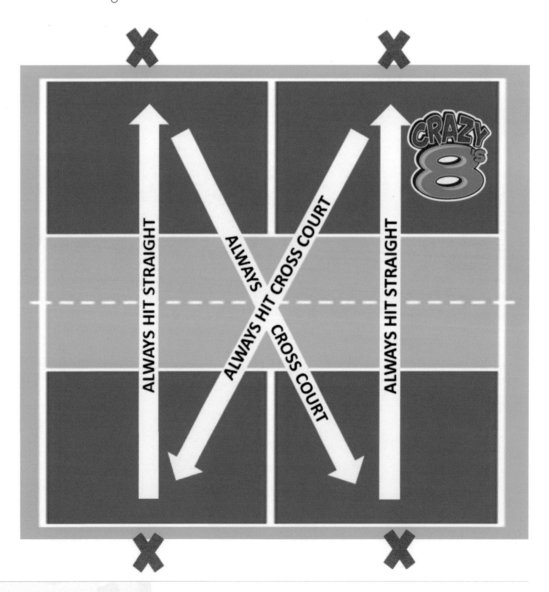

DRILL #35 Skinny Singles Ghost Doubles

Skinny singles and ghost doubles are the best drills you can practice to improve your pickleball game.

Skinny singles and ghost doubles have you practicing your serve, return of serve, moving into the court, working your way through the transition area, and getting yourself to the net.

You will practice split stepping, blocks, resets, and counter attacks.

Once at the kitchen line you can practice dinks, speeding up the ball and lobs. At the kitchen line you can practice punch volleys and moving your opponent around.

Every skill set you will use in pickleball can be drilled with skinny singles.

There is little difference between skinny singles and ghost doubles. Skinny singles, you are always on one side the court. Ghost doubles has you moving from side to side depending on your score.

Receiver	This whole area is out of bounds
Server	This whole area is out of bounds

Ghost doubles is just like skinny singles except your score determines where you stand on the court.

If your score is even, then you will always serve or receive the ball on the even side of the court.

If your score is odd, you will always stand or serve on the odd side of the court.

In this drill you are practicing skinny singles both cross court and straight towards each other, dependent on your score throughout the entire game.

This whole area is out of bounds

Receiver

This players score is odd so they will always be on this side of the court

This players score is odd so they will always be on this side of the court

Server

This whole area is out of bounds

Pickleball Wall Drills

As I travel around the world teaching pickleball to players of all levels, I often get asked how one can drill by themselves.

Sometimes all you have is yourself, a paddle, and a ball. Throw in a wall and you can now train. Fifteen minutes of wall drills is like three hours of playing on the courts.

I have listed several wall drills that will significantly improve your game. Choose a few at a time or go through all thirty. Everyone will be a benefit to your game.

Getting better at any activity is a matter of regular practice and drilling. I understand that drills can be quite boring because you're drilling the same shot hundreds of times, but that's exactly what you need because it helps train muscle memory.

The more you drill, the more efficient you'll be.

Here are a few wall drills that will help take your pickleball playing to the next level. Let's jump right in.

Drill #1   Forehand Dinking

Drill #2   Backhand Dinking

Drill #3   Forehand/Backhand Dinking

Drill #4   Windshield Wiper Forehand Dinking

Drill #5   Windshield Wiper Forehand/Backhand
                Alternating Dinking

Drill #6   Forehand Volley
Drill #7   Backhand Volley
Drill #8   Forehand/Backhand Volley
Drill #9   Windshield Wiper Forehand Volley
Drill #10   Windshield Wiper Backhand Volley
Drill #11   Windshield Wiper Forehand/Backhand
                Alternating Volley

Drill #12   Forehand Reset Volley
Drill #13   Backhand Reset Volley
Drill #14   Forehand/Backhand Reset Volley
Drill #15   Windshield Wiper Forehand Reset Volley
Drill #16   Windshield Wiper Backhand Reset Volley
Drill #17   Windshield Wiper Forehand/Backhand

Drill #18   Forehand Dinking Attack
Drill #19   Backhand Dinking Attack
Drill #20   Forehand/Backhand Dinking Attack
Drill #21   Windshield Wiper Forehand Dinking
Drill #22   Windshield Wiper Backhand Dinking
                Attack

Drill #23   Windshield Wiper Forehand/Backhand Alternating Attack
Drill #24   Serving Drills

Drill #25   Groundstroke drills Forehand

Drill #26   Groundstroke drills Backhand

Drill #27   Groundstroke drills Alternate Forehand/Backhand

Drill #28   Serve/Drop Shot/Dink/Attack/Reset/Dink

Drill #29   Dink/Attack/Reset/Dink/Attack/Reset

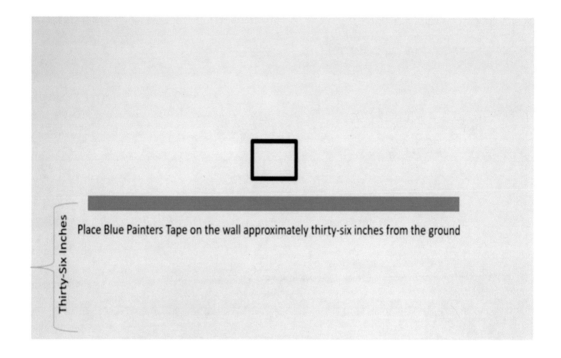

Place Blue Painters Tape on the wall approximately thirty-six inches from the ground

Thirty-Six Inches

Just like in a game, you must expect that every ball in pickleball is coming back at you.

The nice thing about a wall is that every ball does come back.

Stand approximately seven feet from the wall. Your goal is to aim for the center box above the blue line that represents the net.

Set a goal of between twenty-five to fifty forehand dinks. Try and hit the center of the square as a target area.

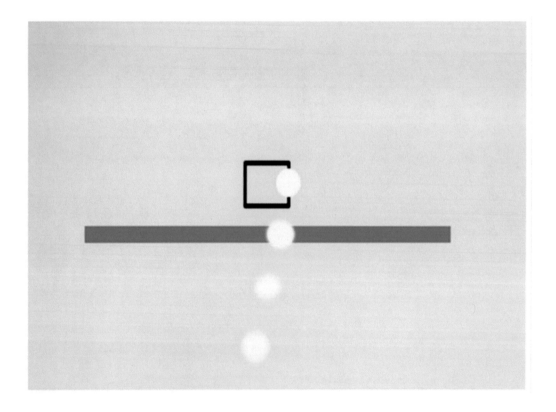

Each of the yellow balls represent the path of your dink.

Backhand Dinking (Drill #2)

Stand approximately seven feet from the wall. Your goal is to aim for the center box above the blue line that represents the net.

Set a goal of between twenty-five to fifty backhand dinks. Try and hit the center of the square as a target area.

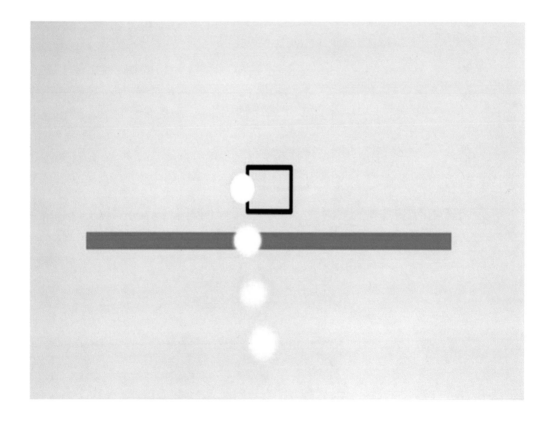

Your first strike is a forehand dink, then your second strike is a backhand dink. Alternate back and forth from forehand to backhand.

Set a goal of between twenty-five to fifty backhand dinks. Try and hit the center of the square as a target area.

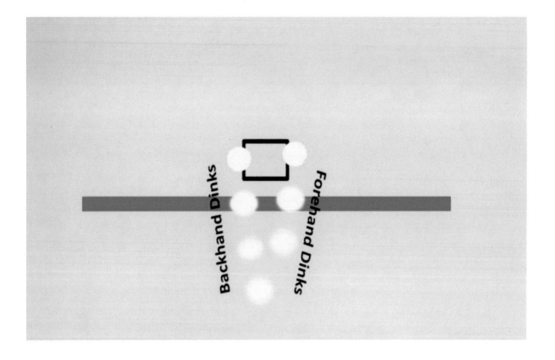

Each of the four yellow balls represent the path of your dink.

Windshield Wiper Dinking (Drill#4)

Stand approximately seven teet from the wall. Your goal is to aim for the center box above the blue line that represents the net.

The goal is to dink and move, Dink, and move. Try and imagine a square box just above the net. Each strike is with your forehand. When you get to the end, work your way back hitting with your backhand.

Set a goal of between twenty-five to fifty dinks. Try and hit the center of the square as a target area.

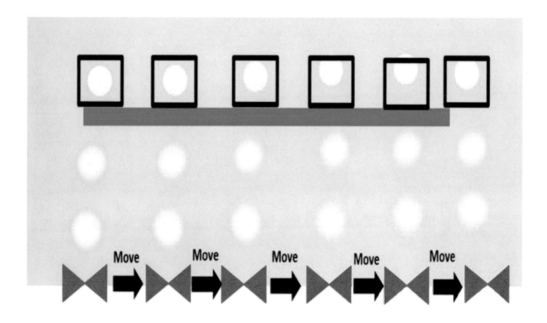

Each of the three yellow balls represent the path of your dink

Windshield Wiper Forehand/Backhand Alternating Dinking (Drill #5)

The goal is to dink and move, Dink, and move. Try and imagine a square box just above the net.

Each strike is with your backhand, then your forehand, alternating. When you get to the end, work your way back.

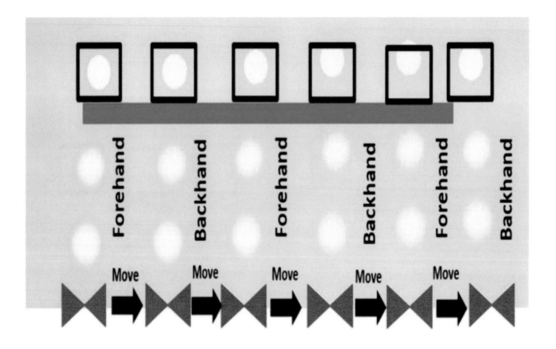

Each of the four yellow balls represent the path of your dink.

Block Volleys, Punch Volleys, Swing Volleys

Any time you hit the ball out of the air, it is a volley. Volleys can be defensive as when dealing with bangers and resetting balls or offensive when taking advantage of higher balls and attacking.

A block volley is when you literally move and freeze, blocking the ball. Make your entire body strong like a wall with a relaxed grip.

A block volley might be used often as resets or when dealing with bangers.

If your opponent is at the baseline and drives the ball to you when standing at the kitchen line, a block volley might be used.

Simply keeping your paddle, a little open, blocking the ball will cause it to float over the net while your opponent is at the baseline.

Often when attacked at the kitchen or in the middle of the court, you might use a block volley as a defensive move to get the ball back over the net.

I often call the block volley the "O crap" volley. The ball is coming at you so fast and unexpected, all you can think about is "O crap" and defend it.

A punch volley is when you have time to punch the ball back. Most likely your punch volley will be with your backhand. I always say, "If you have time to move, you have time to punch"

When you punch volley, you do not have bring your paddle back, it is mostly lifting your paddle up and punching using your shoulder.

A swing volley happens when you have plenty of time to attack the ball. Your entire arm is swinging at the ball. I feel that if you have time to swing you have time to punch.

A punch volley is going to give you better results than a swing volley. Think of how many times the ball was up in the air, you took a big swing to put it away and you hit it out of the court or into the net.

Repeat sessions number one through five. Instead of dinking you will not allow the ball to bounce on the ground.

When you volley the ball, keep your eyes forward. You are not just looking at the ball but the target on the wall you are aiming for. This target might be the open space between your opponents on the opposite side of the net.

If you want your volleys to be slower, then hit the ball higher over the tape that represents the top of the net. If you want the volley to come back faster, hit closer to the tape. The key to volleys is short strokes punching outward. Both backhand and forehand. Make sure your grip is relaxed, not more than a five or six on a scale of ten.

If you find that you overhit, your paddle will not be ready by the time the ball comes back to you.

In this exercise we are practicing our resets as well as our volleys. Repeat drills one through six. When the ball returns to you, open your paddle so the ball rises upward just in front of you so you can hit it a second time as a volley.

This drill forces you to relax your grip, open your paddle face, and punch volley. Three great techniques for effective resets and volleys.

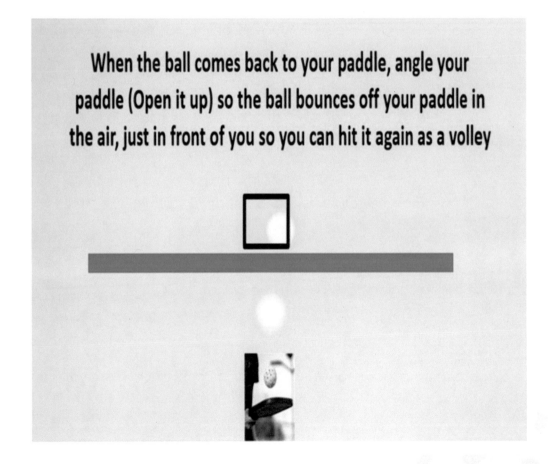

When the ball comes back to your paddle, angle your paddle (Open it up) so the ball bounces off your paddle in the air, just in front of you so you can hit it again as a volley

Attacks from the kitchen line (Drill 18-23)

Disguise your attack at the kitchen line by pretending to dink, and suddenly speed up your follow through. Imagine your dink goes over the net at ten miles an hour. Now increase it to thirty.

It is the change of pace (speed) on the ball that throws your opponent off guard. If your opponent keeps his paddle down, a good target would be their stomach area.

Another good attack area would be the right or left shoulder depending on if they are right or left-handed.

A couple of things to remember when attacking. The first is not to telegraph your attack.

Players will telegraph their attack by bring back their paddle. Just pretend that you are dinking and speed up the ball.

Expect the ball to come back. The purpose of the attack is not to win the point.

The purpose of the attack is to expect the ball to come back where you can put it away.

Do not attack for the sake of attacking. Wait for the right opportunity before you attack.

Repeat drills number one through six but now incorporate an attack.

In drill number one you will dink, dink, attack. You might dink, dink, dink, attack, dink. Mix it up as in a real game.

Stand about ten to fifteen feet from the wall and practice hard deep serves. Practice your pre-serve ritual. What do you do before you serve the ball? Take your time. Breathe. Visualize where you want the ball to go.

Make sure your paddle is just behind your hip. You do not need a big back swing. Bend your knees. Use your legs and torso. Watch the ball contact your paddle.

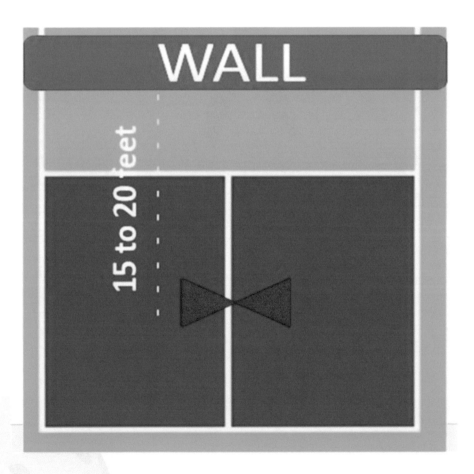

Groundstroke drills Forehand (Drill #25)

Like drill number 25, Stand about ten to fifteen feet from the wall and practice good ground strokes with your forehand. The key is to prepare your paddle as soon as possible.

Working on paddle preparation can be a major game changer for you.

Groundstroke drills Backhand (Drill #26)

Like drill number 25, Stand about ten to fifteen feet from the wall and practice good ground strokes with your backhand. The key is to prepare your paddle as soon as possible.

Working on paddle preparation can be a major game changer for you.

Groundstroke drills Alternate Forehand /Backhand (Drill #27)

Like drill number 25, Stand about ten to fifteen feet from the wall and practice good ground strokes with your forehand, then alternate with your backhand.

The key is to prepare your paddle as soon as possible. Get into a semi closed stance (Turn sideways) whether it is a forehand or backhand.

The key is to prepare your paddle as soon as possible. Working on paddle preparation can be a major game changer for you.

Serve/Drop Shot/Dink/Attack/Reset /Dink (Drill #28)

We start to put it all together now. Stand about fifteen feet from the wall and serve.

Come forward, split step and drop the ball over the net as a third shot drop.

Then dink a few times and attack when you find yourself balanced and in a good position to attack.

After the attack, reset the ball from a volley and dink again.

This is a great workout and simulates much of pickleball.

Dink/Dink/Attack/Reset/Dink/ Attack /Reset/Dink (Drill #29)

In this drill you are staying at the kitchen line. About seven feet from the wall.

You can dink, attack, reset, volley, etc. Mix it up. Work both backhand and forehand.

The Mindset Of A Champion

Be honest with yourself. How much practice time did you put in before got on the court? How often did you commit to drills?

How effective are your serves, return of serves, third shot drops, drives and dinking? What are your strengths and weaknesses? Only you know the answer to that question.

I practiced, I drilled, I had earned the confidence to win.

I wanted to play better than my opponents and better than my partner. Though I had no issues with my partner making errors, I never wanted to let my partner down.

I hope my partner had the same mental attitude and practiced and drilled as hard as I did.

"I NEVER WANTED TO LET MY PARTNER DOWN"

Think of pickleball as a game of chess

The first few moves of a chess game can be the most important moves you make.

In those moves, you establish your strategy and fight for your place on the board.

In pickleball the first four moves (Serve, Return of Serve, third shot, and Dinking) will establish your place on the court. Winning more points and winning more games.

The Serve

When discussing the serve we must understand the primary purpose of serving and then go deeper. Let us start with the obvious. Serve the ball in the court. That is obvious.

Your skill level will determine the strategy of your serve. We need to explore the options of serving for beginners, intermediate and advanced players.

Serving strategy for beginner players: Aim for the middle of the court which gives you five feet of room for errors on each side.

Serving strategy for intermediate players: Aim for the back third of the court. We will discuss the reason in a moment, but for right now, I want you to serve deep to the back third of the court.

Serving strategy for advanced players: Advanced players can serve to their opponent's backhand, forehand, and jamming them in the middle of the court.

Make your serve count.
The purpose of the serve is to set up your third shot

The Return of Serve

Our second chess move in the game of pickleball is the return of serve. We need to talk about the purpose of the return of serve and where might be the most productive place to return the serve.

The purpose of the return of serve is to get to the kitchen line next to your partner

It is important to understand that the team that gets to the kitchen line first will have the advantage.

If you and your partner are both at the kitchen line and your opponents are back, you should win seventy-five to eighty percent of the time. That is why getting to the kitchen line balanced and in position is so valuable.

If you federal express your return of serve, it will federal express back. What that means is, the faster your ball goes over the net, the faster it comes back to you. Will that be enough time to get next to your partner balanced and ready?

If your return of serve is slow and lofty, it gives you time. A soft lofty deep return of serve gives you the time to get to the kitchen line, join your partner, be balanced and be ready to defend any third shot effectively.

We are going to break the myth that the third shot needs to be a drop.

One of the biggest misconceptions is that the third shot needs to be a drop shot. That is simply not true.

Let us start with the highest probability. The third shot should be returned to the player that hit the ball to you.

You and your partner now know, who will be receiving the third shot and which direction the ball will be hit. The only question is whether the third will be a drop or a drive.

What determines if it is a drive or drop? The answer depends on where your opponent is. It is likely a drive and here is why.

1. If your opponent returns serve from the baseline and stays at the baseline admiring their serve. **Drive your third.**
2. 2. If your opponent returns serve from the baseline and stays at the baseline judging whether to stay or move. **Drive your third.**

3. If your opponent returns serve and stops in the middle of the court. **Drive your third.**

4. If your opponent returns serve and is still moving through the middle of the court. **Drive your third.**

5. If your opponent returns serve and barely makes it to the kitchen line. **Drive your third.**

6. If your drops are not working. **Drive your third.**

7. If you are hitting against the wind. **Drive your third.**

8. If you are hitting on your heels. **Drive your third.**

9. If your opponent cannot manage drives. **Drive your third.**

Even if my opponents get to the kitchen line balanced and ready, I will drive at them early in the game to test them and see how they manage drives.

Once I realize that my opponents can manage drives when at the kitchen, my third shot becomes a drop.

I drop the third to the player that returned the ball to me, and I drop it in front of my partner.

When my partner knows that I am hitting the third shot, they are two or three steps ahead of me.

They will get to the kitchen line before me and will be ready to attack if my opponent pops the ball up.

The myth that the third shot needs to be a drop is just that. A myth.

It is ok to drive your 3rd.

The fourth and final critical move in pickleball is dinking. Finally, all players get to the kitchen line and the dinking game begins. Let us start with the purpose of dinking.

The purpose of dinking is to irritate your opponent.

The purpose of dinking is to irritate your opponent. Make them reach and stretch and move to the ball. No longer do you give your opponent easy dinks.

There are two major areas to hit too. Especially at the lower skilled levels. I know there are more areas to attack but this really works. The answer is your opponent's backhand. If I am at the kitchen line and we are dinking, I am dinking to their backhand.

Hit to your opponent's back hand for better results

Stop playing to win...

If you want to become a better pickleball player, you must stop playing to win.

We all want to win; I mean who really likes to lose? To become a better pickleball player you must be willing to lose to get better.

The best players achieved their success simply because they lost more games than you.

One of the biggest mistakes' players make in social play is they play to win the game rather than improve their skill set. What are the areas of your game that you would like to improve?

Use each game as an opportunity to practice that skill set until you feel confident that you can consistently.place that shot.

There are so many things to think about when hitting the ball. Which side of the court should you hit to, should you hit the ball hard or soft, should the ball go deep, or would a shallow drop shot get better results?

Where are the opponents on the court, where the heck is your partner? How can anyone calculate all these algorithms on the court at the same time and return the ball with any sense of direction?

Remember driving a stick shift car for the first time? Your left foot had to push down on the clutch then release slowly upward at the exact time you pushed down with your right foot on the gas pedal.

As if this balancing act was not enough you had to shift gears at the same time. If you were off just a little you popped the clutch and stalled the car or worse, you heard the gears grinding and screaming to be released simply because your timing was off. Left foot down right foot up, right hand shifting, it was like doing the Hokey Pokey.

Then you had to make sure you did not run anyone over as you drove away.

You had to really concentrate but soon you were shifting gears with ease, smoking a cigarette with one arm out the window, changing the radio station and talking to your friend on the cell phone.

At first changing your strategy on the court from winning the game to improving your skill set will have the same affects. It might take effort at first.

It might be painful for a bit. Soon it will all be effort less and your motions and shots will come with ease without you thinking of what to do. You will just do it.

Stop hitting the ball just to return it over the net.

Every time the ball reaches your paddle you should be asking yourself "Where do I want this ball to go?" Where would you like the ball to land? Which side of the court are you trying to place the ball?

Do you want the ball to land deep in the opponent's court or shallow? What I am saying is "Hit the ball with purpose" Do not just send it back over the net.

Become the player that hits with a purpose. Become a player that is willing to lose more now so you can win more later.

Brett Noel is 3x National Gold Medal winner.

Thank you for Investing in yourself and the sport of pickleball.

As a professional pickleball instructor, I have had the privilege of traveling the world teaching pickleball to thousands of players just like yourself.

I have learned many of the shortcuts that can help players advance to the next level, and I incorporate these shortcuts and golden nuggets into my pickleball training camps.

If you would like to have a pickleball training clinic in your area, please reach out to me at BrettNoel2@gmail.com or text me at 805-975-5781

We offer one-, two- and three-day clinics. Each clinic will review everything you need to play better pickleball.

1. Dinking and strategies forcing your opponent to make more unforced errors.
2. How to drop the ball from anywhere on the
3. court
4. How to deal with bangers
5. How to serve and return service as a weapon
6. Effective attacks from the kitchen
7. Pickleball strategies and techniques to win more games.

8. How to drive the ball with power and accuracy
9. Lobs, when to lob and how to defend lobs

    And much more!

Follow me on social media.

Website

www.PickleballSportsllc.com

Facebook

www.Facebook.com/pickleballsportsllc

Instagram

www.Instagram.com/pickleballsportsllc

Twitter

www.Twitter.com/pickleball_llc

Tik Tok

www.tiktok.com/@pickleballsportsllc

Pinterest

www.pinterest.com/pickleballsportsllc

YouTube

Youtube.com/channel/UCFqE3M_V0Ne1HiJRQW0rQyg

"Pickleball is not just a
Sport."
"It's a way of Life."

For FREE Updates on
new drills, strategies, and
techniques, email me at
BrettNoel2@gmail.com

PERFORMANCE PICKLEBALL

Over 60 pickleball drills to accelerate your performance on the courts

Includes 24 wall drills

BRETT NOEL

3X NATIONAL GOLD MEDAL WINNER

Made in United States
Troutdale, OR
09/27/2024

23183678R00069